Believe on fantasy

- Poonam kodwate

Contents

THIS BOOK CAN HELP to knows about universal laws

Everyone gone through that age where we used to be children. When we was children we are living more fullest life than today. We don't had any fear of losing but as we grow up, we tend to have lot of fear in our mind like worry about future , worry about money, worry about relationship and more. Now most of the people wants to return to childhood life because everyone wanted to live joyous life. In childhood life was full of possibilities no fear, no worries. What happen if worry and fear will not existed in world. What happen if there is no thing like money and everything is free in

world then what would you do, what would you add in your cart. What kind of home will you choose to live ? Which car will you choose ? Where trip you will take ?   describe it on paper, write everything. These is the things you want in life. We choose our choices on the basis of money. Money gives us choice. The money we think is not money that is a peace of paper that published by government and they called it money. Money we received is reward for service we give. More we can give service the more money we can have, the more money
we have the more we can do. Now think about money how much do you want to earn? Thinking is the first step to create things. And your first step is done toward your want by thinking about it. Your want is your dream and if you thinks about your dream over and over

it becomes your desire. If you can think it, you can achieve it. Belief is a key to open the door of your want and you can have these key by studying this information over and over. It will raise your belief and awareness.

Chapter 1

NEUROPLASTICITY

Human brain is the most complex structure in the entire universe. Brain is far beyond what computer do. Neurons are the fundamental units of the brain and nervous system. Neurons communicate with each other through electrical signaling these neural connection called NEUROPLASTICITY. NEUROPLASTICITY is a process.   Its changes physiology. Every thought makes neural connection and every movement body makes neural connection in brain. Whatever you do reading, writing or watching our brain makes some connection. Outer physical world you see through eyes is just the reflection of inner circuits of your brain. If you don't like something in your life it just a inner circuit of brain. You and I can change inner circuit and by changing inner circuit we change our outer reality. Inner circuit is just a thoughts and belief we have in our mind. Our circumstances is just a reflection of whats happening in mind . Mind thinking all the time every second so we are creating things all the time through our thinking. If we think negative we are creating negative and it express in our reality. Brain has 70,000 to 80,000 thought every day. 80 % thought were negative and 95 % were exactly the same repetitive thoughts as the day before. Every thought is a brain circuit, if we change thought, circuit will change. Brain is constantly changing, old connections are continually breaking and new ones forming. 70 % of brain connection change every day. Mind have ability to create new images and when mind create image its actually strengthening new circuits in the brain that's how whatever images mind can see, it reflect to outer world. You are the results of these neuron pathways. We can change results by changing these neural pattern of brain. Everything in body is always about chemicals. Imagination is the future. imagination is the fuel of creativity. imagination is our brains ability to form concepts,ideas, images and sensations internally. Every creation on planet start with a dream. There is no really without a dream. Dreams is a series of pictures which is happening in mind and these ability to create mental pictures called imagination. Imagination is the starting point of all achievement. Everything you see in this world came from imagination. Every painting, movie, mobile phone, table, plane, camera first created in imagination. Einstein said, "imagination is everything. It is the preview to life`s coming to attract."imagination more important that knowledge. Knowledge could be great, imagination greater. If you can think it you can do it. If you can imagine your dream life you can achieve. When we focus our thoughts and emotions on what we want to manifest we are actually strengthening the neural connections in our brains that correspond to those desires. Manifestation is a thoughts becomes reality. we can choose thoughts and thoughts create our life. As we think we attract.

Law of Mentalism :   Our world existed only in mind. If we have positive mindset we attracted positive circumstances and situations in life. And with negative mindset everything appear to be negative. Change the root change the fruit.

   Assignment : when mind think negative shift it to think positive and good to attract good.

Law of attraction

Everything in the universe works on the law of attraction. Everything that's comes into our life we have attracted. The law of attraction is a philosophy suggesting that positive thoughts bring positive experiences, events and all results into a persons life, while negative thoughts bring negative outcomes. Law of attraction is not just a belief or a philosophical concept - it is a scientific principle rooted in the neural pathway of the brain.   thoughts are a form of energy and that positive thoughts of energy attracts success in all areas of life, including health, finances and relationship. law of attraction is always be here before we born. Most people attract they don't want rather than what they do want. Because when we think about we don't want, it is a thought and we attract what we think about.

Assignment : Make a habit to think and talk only what you want and don't spend a single minutes on thinking about you don't want.

Law of thinking

Mind is very powerful force in the world and thinking is the very powerful form of energy. Thoughts are things, thoughts are seeds, your dreams are thought when you think about it you are making neural connection and that will reflect in life. thoughts rule the world. Everything in universe is energy and thought is very powerful form of energy. Whatever you want is existed all time. thoughts create your life. As you think you attract. When we think on something its grow. Scientists tell us that thought is compared with the speed of light. Thought travel at the rate of a hundred and eighty six thousand miles per second. Thought travels nine hundred and thirty thousand times faster than the sound of our voice no other force or power in the universe yet known is as great or as quick. that's why you may experience, when you think about something someone near you talk about that. Or if someone wanted to talk something that thought flash in your mind before they say. Thought is invisible to the physical sight it is an actual force of substance. You can flash your thoughts right around the globe several times in less than a single second. We don't have to worry about changing whats going on outside. Thoughts control feelings and feelings control emotions and emotion make you take action and action produce results. For change your result in life we need to change our thoughts. Everything in life is begin to change as you take over the power of thought. The thoughts that you think and turn to your emotional mind instantly by law control the vibratory rate of your body. Body is massive magnetic energy. What you think is going to dictate what this body is going to do. The thought you think repeatedly become fixed in your subconscious mind. And those thoughts are going to determine what happen in your life. Body hear every thought you have. We can have only one thought at a time. What we think produces the result in life.

What kind of lifestyle do you want to live ? whats your vision about your life.

vision

Vision is a long range view of things that you want in your future, that all kind of things you able to see with your minds eye. Tell life what you want. Its very important to know where you want to go and what kind of life you want to live in all area with clarity like what kind of home do you like to live, car and money. Dream car, home are energy and everything in universe is energy. Money is energy and we buy energy with our cash. One rupees have different energy and hundred rupees have different energy. How much money do you want to earn ? Make a vision about your life?. If you don't have vision you missing something in life. If that dream you are holding in your mind that is possible to achieve.

Assignment : Collect the picture of what kind of life do you want to live and make a vision board.

Make a mental movie and see it in mind over and over.

What about your dream home ? build picture of your dream home see yourself you are living their. And who is living with you.

The trip you want to take ? where you are going, see in mind and see who is with you
The business you want to build ?

Or Anything you want ?

Whatever mind can see ,mind can achieve.

Dreams without goals are just goals. Without goal or vision there is no direction. not only imagine but you can actually interpreting your vision through the words. The most important step in achieving our goals and dream is to write them down. By writing that goal we can builds stronger neuronal pathways in the brain and we gave a stronger communication between ourselves and the infinite source.

When we write down ours goals on a peace of paper we have a much greater chance of not only remembering them but we have impressed them into your subconscious mind. By writing goal mind become more clear and clear.

Assignment : Write down your goal in words like you already have it.

Example :

I have(write anything you want in present tense)____________ and I am so happy for it I love it.

Or

I am so happy and grateful now that I am_________ (write your goal in present)

Or

I am so happy and grateful now that I am now earning________ Dollar/ Rupees in week / Month/ Year.

You will become clear the act of writing it down and it will change what you put your attention and it will change your awareness about opportunities to achieve that goal. Writing causes thinking , thinking creates an image. And image building a vision in your mind. Visionaries change the world.

Write your goal like you already achieve that goal because we don't attract what we want we attract what we are. When we think it in present and we have it already we become that person.

Don't try to change outer result without changing yourself. The moment we choose to change our thinking and our emotions, we change the energy that we radiate into our world. Thoughts and emotions impact the chemicals that regulate our mind. This is the law of human functionality. Belief creates life experiences. Every experiences and circumstances in our life is just a belief we have. Thoughts create things, We are creating everything by thinking, we are creators. We are progressive beings you and I. The mind is the basic factor governing the entire life.

Thoughts and emotions impact the chemicals that regulate our mind. You are the results of these neuron pathways. This process of NEUROPLASTICITY allows us to rewire our brains and create new patterns of thought and behaviour , which in turn can attract the experiences and outcomes we desire. Habit is just a neural pathway and if habits you don't like you can change it, with intensity and repetition. We can replace old pathway to new pathway. construct it. A structural change in brain is belief. Belief attracted the event.

CHAPTER 2

SUBCONSCIOUS PROGRAMMING

Everything in universe is energy. Energy neither create not destroyed it transform one form to another. Water is one form of energy it can transform into vapour its another form of energy. We can not destroyed it. Thought is energy We can transform negative thought to positive thought. You will attract into your life what you thinking what you imagining, what you feeling and what you repeating. Every word creating future. We are creating our own life by thinking. You and I are the product of our own experiences. and memories and habits. Life event based on belief and experiences. Every human first seven year is download information from environment called hypnosis, the brain of the child under seven is a lover vibration frequency and lower consciousness, that's called theta. Theta is imagination, theta is hypnosis. Nature make us first seven year to learn what kind of program requires live us on planet. You just watch, you watch your parents you watch sibling and community. Baby learn from surrounding and so much negativity existed in surrounding like so much lack and limitation, struggling, fear and more we learn all these from surrounding and subconscious get program by these beliefs. 95 % life comes from those program in the subconscious and it reflect in our life. When new baby born we don't know emotions we don't understand anything we don't know hunger, we don't know cold or heat when we first came in the world and When we need something we experienced that as anxiety and we cry. We start to develop a relationship with the outside world. We don't really have enough language to describe all the emotional states. We learn everything from environment.

After seven year we develop consciousness. Only 5 % life is conscious which is creative. We imagine things by conscious mind. imagination is engine. We attract in life what we think, talk and imagine. Most of the time we always talking about what we don't want and universe don't understand it whatever we think most it may be our want or don't wants, universe bring it in life. Make positive statement for what you want and make habit. Universe always listening. Positive words saying is just like planting seed in the ground. Be aware what you are thinking and believe what you are thinking is going to come in life. Inner world is more powerful than outer world. Outer worlds follows to the inner world. We have to control thoughts to control life.

If you want to be thought alone or you sit in the meditation and you close your eyes you are disconnecting from the your external environment. Your attention is no longer in the outer world because you are seeing less information which is 80 % of information sensory wise comes through your eyes. You are playing music in the background there you put ear plugs in or there silence now you are hearing less information and because of that you disconnecting from your environment putting your body in one place that time neocortex begins to slow its brainwaves down and brain waves move into alpha and in the alpha that's the imaginary world where the inner world is more real than the outer world. Mind can not differentiate between what is real and what is imagine. Whatever mind can see it reflect in physical word. Mind can see only from our sense called eyes and minds eye.

Universe never send disease, sickness, suffering but it happening in life because of unconscious belief programmed in mind.

Brain can divided into two form subconscious mind and conscious mind.

Subconscious mind:

Paradigm is same as programming that you put in your computer. A paradigm is a program in your subconscious mind that controls your all habitual behaviour. Subconscious mind is emotional mind. We feel by subconscious mind. it is habit mind. These mind rules life. when anything doing repetitively it form a habit. Life is all about habit. Habit control life. We can not control the life but we can control the habit. Subconscious mind accept anything. Our 95% of the day runs by these mind and only

2 to 4 percent day operates by conscious mind. Most of the things we are doing doing by habits. Subconscious mind don't have ability to think. life is all about programming our belief and that belief expressing in life. Its emotional mind whatever belief it take it must express in outer world. For changing belief conscious mind play very important role. If we do not have an image of our success in the unconscious mind, achieving consistent success is practically impossible. Subconscious mind must accept anything that's given to it. Its never reject. law of attraction is always working. Its working according to subconscious belief. We can program these mind. Subconscious mind can not differentiate between whats real and whats imagined. Whatever you impress by conscious mind. whether you imagine it ,hear it ,read it, if you get

emotionally involved in it subconscious mind programmed and its become real. Conscious mind is driver to take you to your dream. What do you really want and make a written description of it in the present tense. When we write we gave signal to subconscious mind what we want. Subconscious bring it in life.

Law of vibration

Law of attraction is secondary law. Law of vibration is primary law. The law of nature states that Everything in life is energy and frequency and   Every energy vibrates on a certain frequency. like energy attract like energy. You can only attract what you are in harmony with you. Everything has a vibration. sound is also a vibration. In universe infinite frequencies existed, there is no end to it, and it all existed at a same time. everything have a frequency. Everything is vibrating. You and I vibrating on a particular frequency. In every frequency our emotions or feelings emits. Anger, grief, shame are the lower vibration. Higher vibration are love, joy, appreciation and excitement. Which feeling we have the most we are gonna receive circumstances and opportunities that match that feeling. Everyday you are attracting what you are in harmony with. If you are operating on a negative frequency, you are gonna feel bad. Feeling describe our conscious awareness of the vibration we are in. If you do not feel good, you have ability to change the vibration you are in. Your dream has a different frequency. To achieve your dream or goal you have to go on that frequency. Like radio if you want to play 97.5 FM you have to tune on 97.5 FM its not working on 98.2 FM. To achieve your goal you have to tune on goal achieved frequency. Your dream is on a frequency. You want to achieve goal is different frequency, its lack frequency because want means you don't have that yet and achieved is different frequency. When you start to act like the person you wanted to become and act like your dream achieved then you are on that your goal frequency. When you stay on that frequency for long period of time. You attract it in your life. When you think about your goal like you already achieved it creates image in mind. Through imagination we can change the frequency. Brain is an electronic switching station and our thoughts activate brain cells and control the vibration we are in and the vibration we are in control what we attract into our life. By changing your vibration everything in your world changes.

We can put ourselves into the vibration that we have to be in to attract what you want to attract. You are attracting what you are so if you want to attract anything in your life you have to be that person in mind.   Law of attraction works on unconscious belief not conscious belief. Law of attraction always working, law of attraction respond to the paradigm. Paradigm is subconscious programming. Visualize it with feeling , repeated over and over and over again it will Reprogram mind. You will see the manifestation. Everything in life manifesting itself in life because of matches the vibration it may be good or bad. Repeating affirmation creates result. Use imagination and build the picture you want. And then we hold that picture with the will. So its your job to always engage the highest vibration. Where your attention is your life goes. Whatever you focus on is what your are going to trend to bring into your life. Focus on what you want, focus is energy, what you focus on grows. Change paradigm you start to attract new things. Desire express through the instrument of the body. Because it changes the vibration the body in. Vibration changes the action.

 Everything emit energy your Skin, Bones, Air ,Thoughts, we are physical matter but we are energy. Match the frequency the reality you want. Energy functions on frequency. keep taking action to match frequency and physical actions also which matches to your goal. Discover your belief, recreate your belief. Change start from within. Change the belief change the reality. You have conscious mind and subconscious mind, body is the instrument of the mind. The body moves into action and produces results. The body acts according to the vibration acts in. Your dream is invisible world. Its only one person can see it. Its you. Anything we see outside it was originated inside. We wanna understand how to close that space , between you are now and your dream life. As you think about goal or something you activate brain cells and you vibrates on that new frequency, you visualize your goal about 21 to 90 days everyday then opportunity and ideas start to come in mind and your ways to make that happen our job is to act on that ideas to make it happen. Without taking action nothing going to happen. Every event, every success, every failure will prepare you for that goal.

Conscious mind:

Conscious mind is objective or thinking mind, educated mind. Conscious mind learn by reading self help book watching self development videos. It can only hold one thought at a time. We can not think about happiness and about worries at a same time. The conscious mind is logical mind. We can create the life we want by this mind. Conscious mind is continually observing what is going on around you. Comparison, analysis, deciding is the function of these mind. Conscious mind is creative mind. The conscious mind does not control our actions. Our actions are almost exclusively controlled by subconscious mind.

We see physical world and make it believe. We have to see by minds eye. It will reflect to the outer world. Subconscious mind identifies information from five senses that's see, hear, smell, taste, touch.conscious mind can see, hear smell taste touch. This is for your physical benefits. These help us to see result we are getting. If you are not getting the result you want there is something wrong inside you not outside there. We are literally programmed to live through our senses. Conscious mind also have higher faculties. We have the will, reason, perception, imagination, memory, intuition. By using these higher faculties we can reprogram subconscious mind. We can communicate with infinite intelligence through those instruments. You become what you think about most of the time. Life is all about experience. Life is reflection of subconscious programming. Reprogram mind through higher faculties.

Perception :   You can not hold too many thoughts in mind at once. Its hard to suppress thoughts but its quite easy to introduce thoughts. When you start introducing thoughts and you start thinking of thought as a form of perception there gonna shape what you see. We may not able to change result but we can change perception. Perception is how you see something. You change the way you look at something and it will change completely. Don't look at life the same way everyday. Try and upgrade your view. Look at it from a different point of view, raise yourself. World Changing according to how we think about world. perception creates a reality. We cant hold too many thoughts in mind at once. Its hard to suppress thoughts but its quite easy to introduce thoughts. When we start introducing thoughts and we start thinking that thought. Perception going to shape what we see in outer world. Paradigm controls our perception. We don't see with our eyes we see through eyes. Our perception of time is directly linked to the NEUROCHEMICAL states that control mood, stress ,happiness, excitement. What we think we become. What we think we create. Thinking is a lot like perception. We do not see the world the way it is we see the world according to our instrument that is eye. You are director of your life. You can edit it by your choice and you are always going to be the hero of your own story. But when you accept someone else`s perception you are the villain in your own story. There is on such thing as an absolute truth because every way of thinking is actually flawed. Everyone have different perception and their life taking shape by their perception.

Assignment: Train mind to see the good in every situation. In a negative situation as well.

Memory: Everyone have best memory, nobody have worse memory. There is not such thing like bad memory. Memory is action of data storage. Memory is capacity to use conscious brain to search and pull together information relevant to the situation at hand. By practicing memorized thing we can develop that faculty. Quantum physicist max planck said, "When you change the way you look at things, the things you look at change. "

Intuition : Intuition is gods way of talking to you. Through your intuition you can pick up your vibration. You can not have a question without an answer. When you ask the question yourself answer will come with it. Everyone have energy around them. And we can learn to feel that energy.   As you start talking people around you and you carry on a conversation with you. You can feel the energy that's coming from them. Feeling is the language of the subjective mind. Intuition picks up feeling. Feeling is vibration its tuned into vibration. Intuition always perfect, its never lie

Reason : Conscious mind is intellectual mind, conscious mind have inductive reason and deductive reason. Inductive side of these mind have ability to accept or reject. When inductive reasoning factor is working we are thinking. Thoughts coming us from circumstances, from people, social media. When we locked into the picture we want, we start to attract thoughts and idea that in harmony with our goals and if somebody gives us thought like you can not do that, its automatically rejected because we are not in harmonious vibration with that thought we locked into the picture that we want. These is how we build the dream.

Deductive reasoning side of conscious we are not thinking. Subconscious is deductive. We are not thinking anything here. Whatever happening around it goes subconscious directly . other peoples thoughts are going into subconscious because you are not rejecting them. You getting thoughts of everyone in your area. subconscious is like earth, it doesn't care what you plant but it will grow with your plant. Whatever planted in subconscious is going to grow in your life.

Will: Will gives the ability to hold one idea in the screen of mind to the exclusion of all outside distractions. Will gives the ability to concentrate. Concentration is a powerful mental tool. To protect yourself against negative influences whether of your own making or negative event around you, recognize that you have will power. Shift your focus on positive side. To manifest your desire you have to stay on new frequency. Many time you will came on old frequency (where you are now) by using will power go into the new frequency, use imagination and act like the person you want to become until it becomes habit.

Imagination: We can turn imaginary world into real world. Mind doesn't know the difference what is good and what is bad. What is little and what is big whatever command we give to it, it will express in life. Great thing is that mind doesn't know the difference between the 0 rupees and 100 crore. And mind doesn't know the difference what is imagine and whats is real. By thinking anything over and over its go to subconscious and it become belief it may be good or bad. Life is expression of belief. Imagination pick up what we know.

How result control us :

Present physical result cause us thinking. Thinking produces emotions and emotions expressed through the body through behaviour and its you create more the same and its cycle we are involved in that's repeating over and over its a self doom fulfilling cycles. Here outer reality controls us and we live outside in.

How we can control result :

Present results are there but they are not in control of us, we can originate prosperous thoughts like you have meaningful relationship, we have good health, you have a great business and you get emotionally involved in these prosperous thoughts and that will cause you to move into a vibration that will create the results that you want. we create belief and repeat it over and over it express in outer world. Here we live inside out our life results is in our control.

Law of assumption : When you pray for something believe that you already have it. Feel that you already have it. You need to feel already the feeling that you are now.

Law of resonance : universe doesn't give you what you want. The universe give you who you are. If you want something, it doesn't mean you are gonna get it. The universe will reflect to you what you are. So become that which you seek to be.

Scientific studies in neuroscience particularly in NEUROPLASTICITY or the brains ability to reorganize itself and think differently by forming new connections between neurons can be very helpful.

CHAPTER 3
WORKING WITH THE LAW

Law of action : the law of action requires that you do something to manifest the things you want., you can not manifest the things you want without taking action these law require to let go of our comfort. Manifestation does not work without law of action. you don't have to spend all day building your dreams you have got life you have got all kind of things you are going to be doing. Take one baby step a day because those big goals you have and the achieving of those goals is won or lost in daily baby steps in the direction of that goal. Daily goal achieving produces yearly goal achieving. You don't get that much done just by sitting and wishing for it. Our actions produce our results. If we want to change our results we have got to change our actions. Taking a 3 to 6 action steps every single day in the direction of your dreams. Sense of urgency speed up manifestation. Make a habit of urgency. Visualize dream and when you receiving some ideas in your head but your not acting on it, it will not be manifesting.

The most powerful way to manifest is in experiencing the fullness of the present moment. Behave like you already achieved it act like goal is already accomplished throughout the day. Hold it as true feel it. Because mind only understand present time. If you visualize something in future it will not going to manifest. We have to really do the inner work to make things happen. we are living from our subconscious .

Law of sacrifice

Sacrifice is law that bring nothing but good into your life. Sacrifice is giving up something of lower nature to receive something of a higher nature.   You move something out to make room for the good that you desire. Holly walk said, Discipline is consciously chosen ardently desires and patiently persisted. Discipline is the ability to give ourselves a command and follow it. No one ever becomes great at anything by accident no one can get something for nothing. Working in harmony with laws its such a winning concept. Our want is on higher nature, to move into higher nature we must have to grabs the habit of that higher nature person and giving out the habit of old person.

Law of gestation : law of gender is also called the the law of gender. In this law we working with masculine and feminine energy. Law of gender dictates that for any physical manifestation there has to be unique balance of those energies. If you get an idea that is the feminine power and as you rationalize the idea and put it into action that is the masculine energy. Law of gender decrees that all seeds have a gestation or incubation period. The seed for carrot takes approximately 70 days. The seed for baby or for you or for me is approximately 280 days. All seeds have a gestation period. Ideas are seeds and there is a gestation period we guess on how long it takes to reach the goal. The space between where you are and where you want to go called timeline. We don't know the timeline but we know we can shorten it. We can shorten it through concentration. If we concentrate on goal we are going to shorten that incubation period. Concentration gives more energy.

Law of growth :   **G**rowth is the essence of reaching our potential. Condition yourself to do it now creates sense of urgency.

 Law of consistency : Discipline is the bridge between your goals and your accomplishments, you need to walk that bridge every single day. If you want to change in life first you have to change what you do on a daily basis. Do it consistently over an extended period of time to benefits compound effect style. Ask yourself how can I do better about whatever you do ?   With the daily discipline to do little things consistently compounded overtime extraordinary results.

Law of receiving :

Personal growth program might be if it does not have a spiritual foundation its incomplete.

Giving is the first fundamental law of life, it's the first law of creation. Willingly give and graciously receive. Entire universe is based on a law of circulation, you have got to keep the energy circulating. Before you can receive you have to create a space for it. Create a space for the good that you desire . You must give something, you have to let go of something before you can receive something. We have got to be relaxed if we are gonna help this happen, put yourself in a totally relaxed state. You have to understand these, and you will understand if you continue to read and study it over and over again. By doing these something will click inside of mind. As we increase our awareness our perception of life changes. Only way to receive good give good. Energy is forever moving. What you have got in your life is a reflection of what you have been giving. If you want greater good you have to got to give greater good. We don't have to worry about what we are going to receive. Willingly giving that's the expression of a lot of faith .

Law of success

Napoleon hill said that an educated person is not necessarily a person with a abundance of general or specialized knowledge. Educated person is a person who has so developed the faculties of their mind that they can acquire anything they want. Nature know no failure

Law of supply:

Man never satisfied. Dissatisfaction is actually creative state. We have ability to create images in our mind and as we create the images in mind we controlled the vibration that we are in and that vibration sets up an attractive force. If you holding thoughts lack and limitations that's what you are going to attract. The universe by law can only give you what you put in the order for.

What you putting in the order for. You attract from one infinite source of supply. Its work for every person, every time, every where because life is reflection of subconscious programming. Success is progressive realization of worthy ideas. Brain is constantly changing. Old connections are continually breaking and new ones forming. You can use your conscious mind to shape your unconscious mind by making new circuits. It require consistency. Thinking positive brain makes positive pathway in brain. By forming the habit of thinking positively we creates new neural pathways in the brain the more we do this the more these neural pathways makes in the brain. We can change whatever we want if we rewire ourselves and sufficiently spend time with reinforcement and intensity to replace old negative behavior patterns with new

constructive alternatives. Make conscious choice to reinforce the new behavior so much more than the old behavior. Focus on solution so much more than problems. To change neural pathway it takes a lot of hard work and reinforcement to build that pathways. Brain act like movie it has soundtrack it has visuals and it has emotions. You want to reinforce new behavior start speaking words positive and constructive. Feed mind with the pictures and the dreams that will help you become that person. Act upon it just do it
Say it see it experience it.

Law if increase:
   There is infinite source of supply. If you are going to increase anything in your life you have to raise it. The more grateful you are the more you going to receive. When you

send loving energy to our source of supply you are gonna find that increase is just automatically going to happen. The more you praise what you are doing or the the people that's working with you the more you are going to win. When you put good in anything good going to comeback.

Bob Proctor says, child that's raised with praise grows up very confident, the child with criticism usually struggles throughout the life. Child that's raise with praise goes on to be a great leader and very confident. This doesn't just work with people, Its true with plant life, its true with animal, its true with money, friends its work with all of life. Praise your friend praise what they are doing. Praise changes our observation. Praise changes your perception. Look something good in your family, friends and people around you. When you seeing the good in it then you want to make them aware that you see. If you want to increase in anything in you life begin to praise. Be grateful for whatever you got. See greater good coming. Be relax and open for receive.

Law of rhythm :

Everything in nature has a pattern ups and down. Your heartbeat has a rhythm. Blood goes through your system with a rhythm. You can see the water goes up and down. Flowers open and close. Everything is either growing or dying. Things raise or fall. Everything is energy, energy have frequency and frequency have rhythm. Night fallows days. Everything that goes one way must come back the opposite way. And then the process repeat itself. Winter never follows winter.

Law of compensation:

When someone makes efforts his or her reward may not come back right away at that very moment but it will come sooner or later in some of the other forms. Its not necessary you will receive reward in the form of money. You can give love and get back love or something more than love in return. By helping others you may get back happiness, financial rewards or fulfilling relationship. Think about what you can do to contribute more to the world with your ideas and actions. The law of compensation based on three steps the amount of money or good you receive is going to be in direct ratio to the the need for what you do your ability to do it and the difficulty there is not replacing you. Universe will give you whatever you asked for but you ask in the form of providing service. It works for every person, every time. The amount of money you earn is going to be in exact ratio to the need for what you do, your ability to do it. The difficulty there is in replacing you. Only we to get best result is to improve yourself. If you want to improve your income improve what you doing. If you want to improve what you are doing, study it.

Law of cause and effect : The law of cause and effect also called sowing and reaping. Everything happens for a reason. There is no cause there is no effect. Success leaves tracks. Just follow the tracks of other successful people. Nature is neural. Nature doesn't care who you are your are male or female , black or white, tall or short , you educated or uneducated nature doesn't care. Reward will match to the level of service

you provide. For every action equal and opposite reaction. What you put out you must get back in return. Earn nightingale says "If a person unhappy with his income just examine and reevaluate your service." Reward in life must exact proportion to your service. If you worry about income and future you are concentrating on wrong thing look at the other end concern yourself only about increasing you service. With becoming great what you are, income and your future will take care of themselves. serve first.

Law of reflection : You are the what you think about yourself all day long. Thinking makes the difference. When we think something repetitively every day its became our habitual thinking and behaviour. subconscious is always reproducing according to your habitual mental pattern and then its reflect in our life. We look at circumstances, Outer situation start to form in our mind. Like I don't know how or we don't have time or we have not got any money or I am afraid if I try and I tried something once and lost. People focus on it and they get emotionally involved in it. As they get emotionally involved in it instantly and automatically they move into that physical vibration and it causes action that produces more of the same result. That how you and i trap in cycle.

 When we want to change our reality then first thing to change the thinking. Universal law of reflection is that you will see outside of you what is inside of you and you will attract your mirror to you. Whatever energy give out its always come back, whatever love you give out its always come back if anger give out it always come back. Things we want to change outside we are all reflection of whats going on inside. Your feeling and the thoughts that your thinking you send out a signal an energy that reflects your outer world. You choose your thoughts and thoughts create your life. As you think you attract. You are gonna attract whatever you have not healed in a relationship so more you love you and heal you and know you and listen to you and take responsibility for you and make different choices in your life then you attract the abundance in love, in relationship with money, with career, with vision, you attract

it all because its just a reflection. What choices have I made in life about me and whatever that is what you will attract even if you are unconscious of it you will attract it. You must be responsible to love you, to know you, to heal you. Because like attracts like. Law of attraction is about whatever you put in the world return to you and probably ten fold. Listen to the heart, how you feel about yourself. Universe always working for us is always ready to serve us. We are responsible for our life take full responsibility to our life and take responsibility to change it where needed. Appreciate what you already have. Be looking for the opportunity and take action when you see them. Maintain momentum.   Experiences always reflect your inner belief . look at experiences and determine whats belief are. Look at the people in your life they are always mirroring some belief you have about yourself.   Words shapes the life according your belief. What we gave out in the form of words its return to us as experiences. Outer circumstances of our

life is just effect of the whats going in side conversation. Everything is a manifestation of the mental conversation. Experiences always reflect your inner belief. Look at experiences and determine whats belief are. Look at the people in your life they are always mirroring some belief you have about yourself.
Belief what visualize.

Law of correspondence : Our circumstances are a mirroring of our inner being. So toxic people can be our best teacher. The same type of person will show up again and again until we can not change the inner belief. We can find ourselves in a cycle of repeating the same lesson over an over again until we change our emotions. If you notice something happen many times in your life. That you don't like then Focus on changing your reactions and emotions to change that pattern. Shift focus , your focus and attention matters.

Assignment : Catch up outer situation happening over and over that you don't like write it down in opposite, make a new belief by repeating over and over new belief plant in mind. New belief will grow and old will disappear.

Law of pschological reciprocity : that law states whenever you good put out you will get good back but very rarely right away when you put better dang you get it right back.

Law of reversibility : Prayer is an art and require practice, first require the controlled imagination. The essence of prayer is faith. But faith permeated by understanding.

Law of polarity : There is an opposites for everything and anything in our world. Opposite and the same. You count have right side of your body without left side of body. There is no bad without good , there is top without bottom. There all are opposite side of same thing. Nothing is good or bad, We make it good or bad by thinking . If everything both good and bad then whats in center? is just is. Everything is just is. We choose to look good or bad. Nothing good or bad our thinking will make himself. Doesn't matter whats going in life, we cant control the circumstances but whatever circumstances its either going to control you or you are going to control it , that's your choice. Harvest the good, let go of completely. If you let go of the bad the good seems to grow. you have ability to choose,

choose good. If you choose good you are going to get result good. If you look for good you are going to find it. look only and only good in everything and everyone everyday all day long doesn't matter what happen. You have a choice to say that's good. Doesn't matter what it is. Say that's good. By building positive negative will disappear. Prosperity and poverty are not two things there are merely two sides of one thing the same thing.

Assignment : form the habit of saying that's good.

Assignment : form a habit to look positive and prosperity.

Law of forgiveness :

The body of human move by the mind. Forgive yourself. You cant change what you did. Guilt is very destructive emotions.

Forgive means let go of completely let it go.Forgiveness I very healthy concept. We have got to learn forgive ourselves we have got to forgive others. We have to realize that what we did yesterday we cannot change. If you did something wrong let it go forgive yourself. If someone else has done something to you don't hold any resentment let it go that doesn't mean that you want to go and give them opportunity to do it all over again. You cant hold bad thought in your mind and move in a good direction.   When it comes back into your mind let it go again .

Carrying bad thought about anyone or anything is not doing anyone any good but it buying your income friend company

Forgiveness its gonna cause everything to grow

Its gonna cause you to be healthier its gonna cause your income to grow friends ,business to grow

Assignment :

Form a habit of not holding on to anything that causing you to feel bad.

Assignment :

Start to love yourself, start to respect yourself, have a healthy respect for what you are capable of doing.

Law of non resistance

Resistance is a signal that you are moving into a new area . you and I programmed to resist resistance. Law of non resist whatever you resist persists next time when you meet with resistant rather than fight back just let it go.   Remember don't react respond. Reacting is habit, and to respond you have to think

Law of detachment: " He root of suffering is attachment". attachment comes from poverty consciousness. The law of detachment says we must detach ourselves from the result or outcome in order to allow what we desire to materialize in the physical universe. Let go of outcome and once we let go when things materialize. They may not come the way we expected them to come but they do come. Practicing law of detachment doesn't mean we have to stop putting intentions or stop taking action and to be detached from outcome in order to manifest what we want. When we are detached from the outcome we create space for things to materialize through you. When you are holding on to things we are blocking the space. By detachment we reduce our suffering and stress. By putting you attention on what you can do today, you forget what the outcome was, because outcome is not in your control when you forgetting the outcome you allow for higher and better outcomes to come. Attachment to money always create insecurity. Choice of word creates experiences in life. MARK BORIS the CEO of wizard home loads said that its foolish to plan the long term because things always change. By law of detachment stress level will reduce.

Let go of past. put energy to learning about yourself. What the let go. You will see problem and issue you need to dissolve. Look at the block that block to good things in life. Life is here to support us all the time. Changing our self talk.   The way we talk to ourselves impact in life.   Words attract to us as a experiences. Love and appreciate makes like amazing.

don't hold on to stories that make us small or keeps us small. Sometime we might lose or miss the signs that are there to support us in our path, remember the signs themselves are not good or bad it is our judgement our interpretation that makes them so you have to get clear of the inner blocks in your subconscious. Lack and limitation belief create a block in manifestation. If there is any block anywhere in your life it is most likely due to a lack of forgiveness. You have to forgive yourself and others. Forgiveness is decision to let go of anger and resentment. Buddha who said carrying resentment
around is like carrying a hot coal in your own hand expecting it to burn the other person. It doesn't burn the other person it burns you. If a man wishes someone bad luck. he is sure to attract bad luck himself. Thoughts are

creative. Speak in positive.Choice of word creates experiences in life. Words shapes the life. What we gave out in the form of words its return to us as experiences. Life is here to support us all the time.

Changing our self talk. The way we talk to ourself impact in life.   Words attract to us as a experiences. Let go limiting belief that don't serve you . Unhappiness is self generated in the mind and the reason is because we are attaches to the outcome, if you compare some of your problem to someone else`s problems in a third world country your problem will disappear. To put some positive belief you must let go of these old belief. Let go of toxic people surrounded by you, Our inner voice or self talk can have a devastating effect on our mental and emotional well being. This voice or self talk can keep us stuck in the past

Assignment : put all attention on what you can do today to get closer to where you want to get.

The law of obedience:
  The more obedient I become the more I'm gonna win. understanding only comes through study. You can build wisdom according to your obedience according to your understanding of divine law and the use of it in your daily life. We see in nature of the answer, nature no trouble she can not overcome .

Law of divine oneness: Everything is connected in universe. Every individual are connected. We are one. We are all connected. Everyone of our heart beat is connected.

Law of correspondence : this law states that patterns repeat throughout the universe, and on a personal level, our reality is a mirror of whats happening inside us at that moment.

Law of relativity: don't focus on whats wrong focus on whats right.

Vacuum law of prosperity :

When we make a space for good we desire that going to come. If we don't create the space for good we are not going to get it. You can not put anything where table stand in your room until you get rid of that table. If you want positive things to happen in your life then you have to create space by letting go old negative things. Letting go the old ideas, belief create a space so you can receive good and new idea. If you wanting something then give it away you don't want. These is universal law and these can not change by man.

Law of money :

Money is neutral energy. Money makes a difference in life because money gives ability to choose. Money is tool , we use it to make your dream come true. If you set your desire don't think about money. If your desire is strong money will attract to fulfil that desire. When you keep seeing your want in conscious mind it becomes desire. Money is spiritual tool to make life easy, money cant buy happiness but money can solve those problems arises from lack of money. Everyone have program about money. Money goes where it appreciated.

By Changing belief we can welcome money. Fall in love with money. Universe is bigger and smarter and far more resourceful for that. Be open to receive it from number of ways. When talk bad about wealthy people is actually blocking the wealth to come in life.

Chapter 4
Play with neurons and
NEUROCHEMICALS

Brain is all about chemicals.That chemical help to transmit messages from one brain cells to another one called neurotransmitters. Brains are swimming in NEUROCHEMICAL that is DOPAMINE , SEROTONIN, ACETYLCHOLINE, GLUTAMATE. These chemical make huge impact on our behaviour emotions and thoughts. We experienced good feeling when we laugh that time chemical produce called serotonin which is good. If we stress to much producing chemical act as inhibiting chemicals. They block transmission between cells. Healthy brain is better able to regulate emotions and manage stress which makes it easier to stay positive and optimistic.

Healthy brain maintain a positive outlook even in the face of challenges healthy brain help to avoid negative thinking patterns, its better able to engage in problem solving and creative thinking.

Dopamine

   Very low dopamine creates a state of discouragement , people don't see possibilities in the world. When dopamine at normal level possibilities see everywhere. Dopamine is release when you win a game, someone likes your photo. But most of dopamine release is not from achieving goals its actually released when we are working on our goals to achieve them and we think we are on the right path. Feel some sense of reward. Dopamine is know as the pleasure NEUROCHEMICSL of the brain. Dopamine system is exceedingly powerful because dopamine is a kind of a dumb molecule.   It has no brain of its own. Its just a molecule. Its chemical. But when dopamine release in our brain it motivates toward achieving goals. It's the molecule not just reward but of motivator.   Dopamine is more than a source of pleasure, dopamine is a powerful motivator. Dopamine release is associated with beliefs, when we believe something there are chemical reward systems in our mind. Dopamine reward when we repeat some believe. It also has dark side, the dark side is people very fix in their negative beliefs and they are actually being chemically rewarded for having the same negative belief. When positive belief we have on something dopamine motivates to do that positive things and we go on positive direction. When negative belief we have dopamine reward us to think and do negative. It can take us on negative side as well positive side. It depend on our belief.

Serotonin

Serotonin is a chemical that sends signals between your nerve cells in the brain and throughout body. Serotonin is increase when we are engaged in repetitive behaviour. You experienced good feeling when we laugh that time chemical produce called serotonin which is good. If we stress to much producing chemical act as inhibiting chemicals. They block transmission between cells. Thoughts and emotions impact the chemicals that regulate our mind.

Endorphin

ENDORPHIN are chemicals, body release when it feels pain or stress, endorphin help relieve pain, reduce stress. Body release Endorphin during pleasurable activities such as exercise, massage, eating, romance as well. They are feel good chemicals because they can make you feel better and put us in positive state of mind.

Epinephrine

Epinephrine or ADRENALINE is a molecule that is made from the molecule dopamine. Epinephrine is essentially the basis of neural energy. It gives ability to focus, it gives the ability to alert, it gives the ability to continue working. Epinephrine or adrenaline made from the molecule dopamine. Adrenaline is help you to fight. Its good to know how to fight or fight back.

To feel calmer

- Breathe deeply
- Take a nature walk
- Calming music
- Talk to a friend or relatives.

OXYTOCIN

OXYTOCIN called love hormone. OXYTOCIN increase by hug a person you love, by hug a pet and by helping people. OXYTOCIN is know as cuddle chemical its also reduces stress. OXYTOCIN release during cooking, wood working and gardening.

CORTISOL

Stress hormone called CORTISOL . people in depression because of high CORTISOL level is high.

Maintain CORTISOL level

- Walk in nature
- Exercise
- Living in clean and organized space
- Stay hydrated
- Limit caffeine
- Avoid alcohol
- Healthy diet

Happiness

        Happiness is state of mind. Sometimes happiness also depend on interactions with your environment and social environment. Four main chemicals impact on happiness which is serotonin, dopamine, endorphin and OXYTOCIN. When we are in good company or surrounded by positive minded people our brain releases the chemical OXYTOCIN and DOPAMINE these chemical reduce stress and improve mood.

Habits that help to raise happiness

- Meditation
- Gratitude
- Exercise
- sleep
- Positive self talk

Meditation

Consistently meditation is beneficial that's enhance the ability to focus. 5 min a day meditation can have fairly outsizes positive effects. meditation is focused base training. Even a 5 min a day to 13 min a day meditation can greatly increase our ability to focus and ability to refocus again and again on what we are doing throughout our day. Taking deep breath is way to connect with body.

Benefits of meditation:

1. Meditation enhance focus and directing our focus.
2. Lower your stress.
3. Maintain attention in present moment.

4. We become less caught up in the momentum of negative thoughts about ourselves.
5. Turning our attention and focus away from the arising of negative self talk, this creates the internal space necessary to be able to redirect our thoughts to more positive and beneficial thinking in other words replace negative thought and self criticism with positive self talk.
6. Meditation improve performances.
7. Improve sleep quality.
8. Meditation adjust stress.
9. Meditation practice can shift the brain and body.
10. Meditation can give you very specific results.
11. Help to listen inner voice.
12. Help to reprogram negative belief.

13. Relax body and mind. The more you relax the more we open to receive information.
14. Breath out and release the negativity.

Law of Gratitude

Gratitude is simply the practice of focusing on the things in life that you are grateful for. Gratitude is powerful tool to attract good in life instead of chasing thing. Thankful heart is the state of receiving. When we live in gratitude frequency universe bring all the things in life we are grateful for. Repeated gratitude practice changes the way that brain circuits work. It also change the way in which heart and brain interaction. Brain control heart. Regular gratitude practice could shift the functional connectivity of emotional pathways in ways that made anxiety and fear circuit less like to be active and circuits feeling of well being also motivation to be much more active. If you have a gratitude practice and you repeat regularly you reduce the fear anxiety circuits and increase the positive emotion, feel good circuits. The best time of day to do gratitude practice is when you first wake up in the morning or before you go to sleep at night. Neural circuits and body change by gratitude. It is the frequency of abundance, you shift your vibration by gratitude. It also shift heart rate and breathing. Engaging in gratitude practices there is an increased activity in the PREFRONTAL CORTEX this is the brain region involved in regular emotions and controlling behaviour. Also increases activity in the hypothalamus. You can easily practice gratitude by expressing gratitude to other either through verbal appreciation through act of kindness or just writing down each day what you are grateful for. Neuroscience tells us that expressing gratitude has profoundly positive effect on the brain. Receiving gratitude more powerful than giving gratitude. Engaging in positive thinking and practicing gratitude our brains change activity in certain regions of the brain.

Benefits of gratitude
- Practicing gratitude improves mood
- Reduce stress and anxiety
- Gratitude Enhance mental health.
- Increases our sense of overall well being

Assignment :

Write a gratitude letter to someone you are grateful for, it could be your mother, father,brother,sister ,friend, mentor, partner, any person who make positive difference in your life, to whom you have never fully expressed your thanks or anyone by your choice with a meaning and lot of thoughts behind that letter. When you are write this letter focus on all good things. After you write this letter go to this person and read it to them if possible.

That time you change the neural circuit about that person. Letter can make a big difference to us, it can make a difference to the person receiving it. It can make difference to the relationship

Assignment :
Receive gratitude from yourself. Praise yourself whatever you do.
By doing these you will activate gratitude circuit in your brain and that create sense of joy. It will raise self love and self image.

Exercise

Exercise is a body activity that enhance or maintain physical health.

- Exercise support the growth and maintenance of brain cells and brain health.
- Exercise has also been found to improve blood flow to the brain which can help to support brain function.
- Exercise has a positive effect on mood and emotional well being.
- Help support positive thinking and remember as the law of attraction states positive thought attracts positive outcomes.

Sleep

Sleep is state of rest in which reduced mental and physical activity. Sleep plays a crucial role in consolidating memories and strengthening the connection between neurons in the brain.

- sleep helps improve learning and memory.
- Adequate sleep essential for brain health.
- Sleep Maintain problem solving skill.
- Sleep Maintain decision making skill.
- Sleep Support our capacity for positive thinking.
- Sleep Help to regulate body stress.
- Sleep Reduce negative effect of stress on brain and body.

Lack of sleep causes

- Negatively impact mood and memory and problem solving skill.
- Difficulty managing emotions

Self talk

self talk refers to the internal dialogue that we have with ourselves. The primary strategies for cultivating positive self talk are:
Pay attention to the thoughts you have about yourself and your abilities
When you notice negative thoughts try to recognize them as just thought rather than facts
Replace negative thought with positive thoughts.
Example: I am not good enough to I am doing my best.

Benefits of positive self talk :

- Positive self talk helps to form strong neural connection that leads positive thinking.

- Positive self talk has also increase the production of BRAIN DERIVED

NEUROTROPHIC FACTOR (BDNF). This is a protein that supports the growth and maintenance of brain cells which helps to improve brain function and support good mental health in other world positive self talk makes our brain grow and keeps it healthy.

- practicing positive self talk increases activity in the PREFRONTAL CORTEX this is the region of the brain that is involved in decision making, problem solving and regulating emotions by increasing activity in this brain region. We can improve our mood and greatly reduce stress awakening this region of the brain through positive self talk.

Synthesizing happiness:

Synthetic happiness is self creates happiness or self directed happiness or false happiness. The synthetic happiness is not simply about imagining happiness or thinking about happiness or anticipating happiness. Synthetic happiness is source of happiness as natural happiness. Natural happiness is when we get what we wanted. Synthetic happiness is what we make when we don't get what we wanted. Synthetic happiness is every bit as real kind of happiness. Synthetic happiness is important, it makes happy neural connection and happy chemical in brain. We vibrates in happy vibration frequency and happy frequency is the frequency of receiving.

- Using music or background sound that you find very pleasant combined. Sound is frequency and music take you in good frequency and it feel good

- Doing work that meaningful to you or leading to meaningful outcomes creates happiness.

- The pet and the human receive hug increases in OXYTOCIN and other relate NEUROCHEMICALS that make us feel bonded. Just even seeing a dog for a brief amount of time has been shown to reduce stress and improve happiness or increase feeling of happiness.

- Stay present on what we doing. It is the enormous happiness increasing value of being present to what we are doing.

CHAPTER 5
Make change by making
winning habit

Success is a series of habits you created. Tim ferriss said, if you want to win the day, you have to win the morning but to win the morning first have to win the evening. So you must have a plan what you are going to do tomorrow. its will be so powerful to set 3 to 6 goal achieving goal before go to bed. Without taking any action goal achieving is sometime fail manifestation.

- Make habit to write goal achieving goals every single evening for next day. And become goal achiever.
- When we wake up our mind is so widely open so by waking up and started to scrolling phone will be not the good idea. Replace that habit with morning routine

Steps to start day

1. write goal in present tense.
2. Write ten things you are grateful for.
3. Write twenty 25 I am statement.
4. Meditation or visualize your dream.

5. Study, reading, audio listening 15 to 20 minutes.
6. Exercise
7. Autosuggestion or say your affirmation in front of mirror.

- Practice though out the day focusing on good in everyone and everything.
(When mind focus on good , good attracts to us

 Decision takes by conscious mind but whole work driven by subconscious mind. We can shape life the way we want by Every single day.)
- consciously and intentionally choose thoughts. Universe always send what we choose.
- Build the picture of you already achieved what you want. When you do that you creating new self image.

- Create the habit of that person you
- desire, to create habit you have to create daily discipline, it takes 66 days to create a habit then it becomes automatic.
- Develop attitude of that person. Attitude is a combination of our thoughts, feeling and actions. Make sure our attitude is aligned with the person that you want to be. You have to think feel and act from the person you want to be. Only accept the thought and ideas which is matches to your new self, reject that idea which matches to your old self and not matches to new you.

- Take control of the thoughts that come from conscious mind so you can program that once comes from your subconscious mind so you can live effective life.

- Be conscious of the people you surround yourself with.
- Be conscious what you read.
- Be conscious what you listen to.
- Be conscious about what you say.
- Discipline is the ability to give yourself a command and then follow it. Make committed decision that your going to live like new you and stick on it. When you do that you operating on a completely different frequency.
- Every thought leads us to a feeling and feeling we have makes us move either away from or towards our dream. Feeling leads actions.
- Feel that you already have the good you desire through out the day.
- Read goal and your affirmation at least

10 to 20 times a day. At the moment you say your affirmation immediately you go on new frequency.

- Write down self image over and over.
- There is so much negativity in physical world. We have to master morning and day. Taking committed decision to do 1% better than yesterday that can make huge difference in life.

Whats going on interior is going to show up outside. What are you doing today, what are you doing tomorrow, what are you doing in the next few weeks is gonna dictate what comes to you.

- Aware of your current thinking.

I am not good enough, its not going to work out. Negative thought keep people shut down.   Rebuild software of the mind. The Reticular activating system in the brain.

Responds to repetition imaginary and emotion.

- Man can only receive what he seem himself receiving. Every big accomplishment has been brought into manifestation through holding the vision and Often just before the big accomplishment comes apparent failure and discouragement.

- You can control any situation if you first control yourself. God doesn't need any time and he is never too late. If we want grater good then get rid of old belief.

- First law of learning is repetition. Through repetition subconscious mind learn. But gathering information is not learning, learning is when you implementing information or ideas and get result then you learn something.

- Master your mind and use it intelligently and pray with intention.
- law of attraction is always be here before we born.
- When mind received any idea just do it. Act on ideas. Make a habit of urgency. When idea pop up in mind, do it now.
- Self image controls everything. If you have to grow you have to change, there is no other way. Make habit to update self image everyday.
- Today's self image created the future.
- Quantum physics is the fundamental rule of the universe. Thoughts are electric and emotions are magnetic. The brain and the heart work together creating an electromagnetic field.

Brain is an electronic switching station it controls vibratory rate of this massive energy that we call body. We can control the vibration we are in when we start to control whats comes into our life.

● When we live in the harmony with law we start to win.